LOOK INSIDE
CROSS-SECTIONS
SHIPS

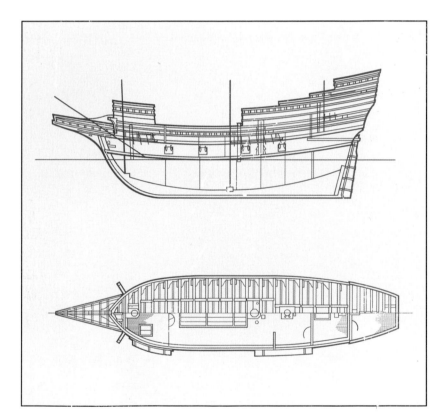

LOOK INSIDE
CROSS-SECTIONS
SHIPS

ILLUSTRATED BY
JONOTHAN POTTER

WRITTEN BY
MOIRA BUTTERFIELD

DORLING KINDERSLEY
LONDON • NEW YORK • STUTTGART

A DORLING KINDERSLEY BOOK

Art Editor Dorian Spencer Davies
Designer Sharon Grant
Senior Art Editor C. David Gillingwater
Senior Editor John C. Miles
Production Ruth Cobb
Consultant John Robinson
The Science Museum

First published in 1994
by Dorling Kindersley Limited,
9 Henrietta Street, London WC2E 8PS

Reprinted in 1995

A CIP catalogue record for this book is available
from the British Library

ISBN 07513-5163-6

Reproduced by Dot Gradations, Essex
Printed and bound by Proost, Belgium

CONTENTS

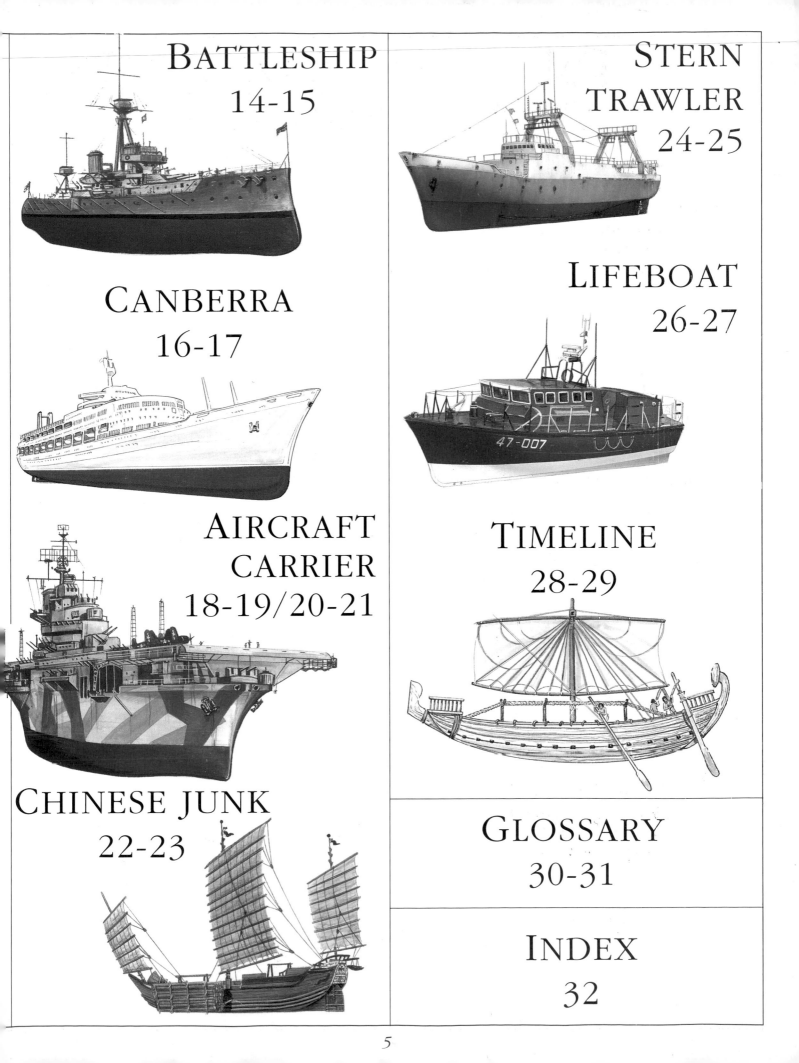

TRIREME

IMAGINE A FLEET of fast narrow ships coming
towards you, each one with a set of fearsome eyes painted on the front.
You would hear the splashing of oars and see swords glinting in the sun. If
you were an enemy of Ancient Greece the sight would fill you with fear. These
ships were called triremes. They belonged to the powerful nation-state of Athens
about 2,400 years ago. As yet no-one has found any remains of a trireme. However,
it's possible to work
out what they looked
like by studying pictures
on Ancient Greek vases
and carvings, and a trireme
reconstruction has recently been built.

*Boatmast yard
supports sail*

Boatmast

Boatsail

Carved prow

Masts and sails
There were two trireme masts
and sails – a mainmast and a
mainsail amidships (in the
middle) and a boatmast
and boatsail forward.

Strike sails!
Normally if a trireme went into
battle the sails were left on land and
the masts were taken down and laid
in the boat. This trireme has been
attacked by surprise so the masts
and sails are still up.

The business end
At the bow (the front)
there was a platform
where a ship's officer
(called the *Prorates*) sat,
together with some crew
members. He took orders
from the helmsman.

*Bow
platform*

Hoplites *were
heavily
armoured
soldiers*

Zygian (*middle
row oarsmen*)

Lance

Bow officer (Prorates)

*Painted eye to keep
bad luck away*

Ram raid
Triremes were designed to
ram enemy ships and hole
them below the waterline.
The ram had sharp teeth.

*Fighting
platforms*

Underwater ram

Danger! Splinters!
There were 170 oarsmen on
board, each pulling a heavy
oar. They rowed in time to
music played by a piper.

*Thalamian
(bottom row
oarsmen)*

*Keel of oak
wood*

*Thranite
(top row
oarsmen)*

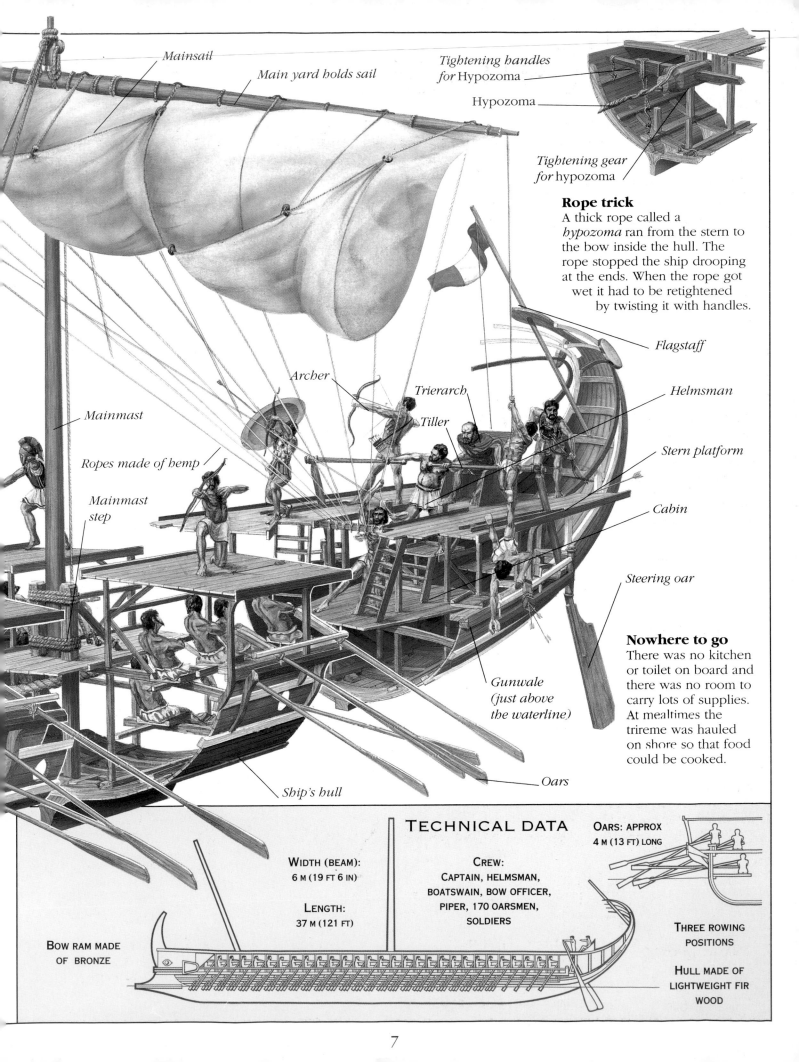

Mainsail

Main yard holds sail

Tightening handles
for Hypozoma

Hypozoma

Tightening gear
for hypozoma

Rope trick
A thick rope called a
hypozoma ran from the stern to
the bow inside the hull. The
rope stopped the ship drooping
at the ends. When the rope got
wet it had to be retightened
by twisting it with handles.

Flagstaff

Archer

Trierarch

Helmsman

Tiller

Stern platform

Mainmast

Cabin

Ropes made of hemp

Mainmast
step

Steering oar

Nowhere to go
There was no kitchen
or toilet on board and
there was no room to
carry lots of supplies.
At mealtimes the
trireme was hauled
on shore so that food
could be cooked.

Gunwale
(just above
the waterline)

Oars

Ship's hull

TECHNICAL DATA

OARS: APPROX
4 M (13 FT) LONG

WIDTH (BEAM):
6 M (19 FT 6 IN)

CREW:
CAPTAIN, HELMSMAN,
BOATSWAIN, BOW OFFICER,
PIPER, 170 OARSMEN,
SOLDIERS

LENGTH:
37 M (121 FT)

BOW RAM MADE
OF BRONZE

THREE ROWING
POSITIONS

HULL MADE OF
LIGHTWEIGHT FIR
WOOD

MARY ROSE

ON A SUMMER'S DAY in 1545 Henry VIII of England sent his best warships to defeat a French fleet threatening his kingdom. The mighty *Mary Rose* was among those ships sailing out of Portsmouth that day. Suddenly, she rolled over onto her starboard (right) side. Water rushed into her open gunports and she sank like a stone. Nearly 700 men drowned before the gaze of the shocked onlookers, including the King, watching on land from nearby Southsea Castle. The *Mary Rose* lay on the seabed for 437 years before her hull was raised and brought ashore. When she was rediscovered divers found hundreds of items that provided a unique record of life on board.

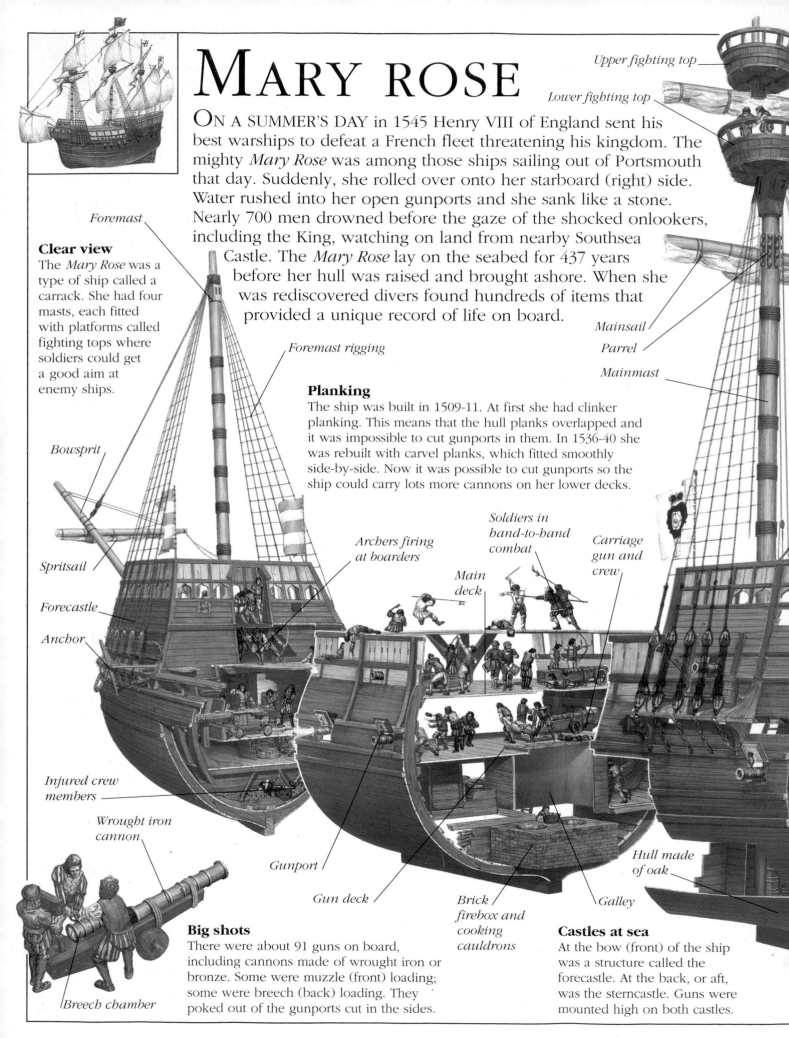

Upper fighting top

Lower fighting top

Mainsail

Parrel

Mainmast

Clear view
The *Mary Rose* was a type of ship called a carrack. She had four masts, each fitted with platforms called fighting tops where soldiers could get a good aim at enemy ships.

Foremast

Foremast rigging

Planking
The ship was built in 1509-11. At first she had clinker planking. This means that the hull planks overlapped and it was impossible to cut gunports in them. In 1536-40 she was rebuilt with carvel planks, which fitted smoothly side-by-side. Now it was possible to cut gunports so the ship could carry lots more cannons on her lower decks.

Bowsprit

Spritsail

Forecastle

Anchor

Archers firing at boarders

Soldiers in hand-to-hand combat

Main deck

Carriage gun and crew

Injured crew members

Wrought iron cannon

Gunport

Gun deck

Brick firebox and cooking cauldrons

Galley

Hull made of oak

Breech chamber

Big shots
There were about 91 guns on board, including cannons made of wrought iron or bronze. Some were muzzle (front) loading; some were breech (back) loading. They poked out of the gunports cut in the sides.

Castles at sea
At the bow (front) of the ship was a structure called the forecastle. At the back, or aft, was the sterncastle. Guns were mounted high on both castles.

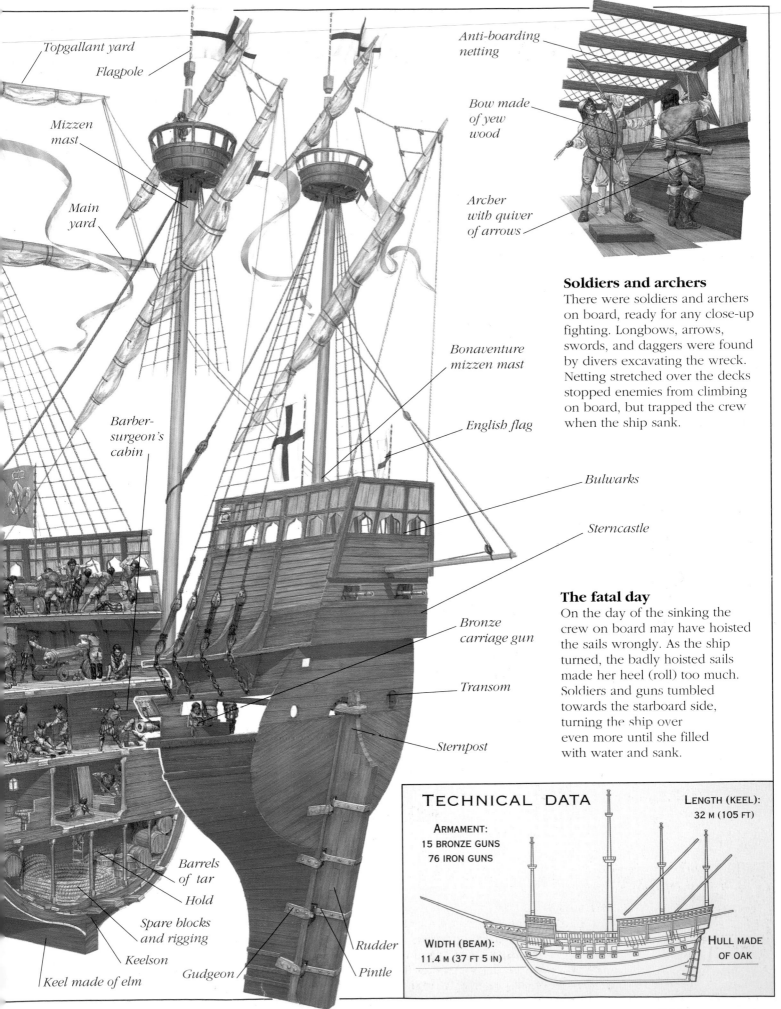

Topgallant yard

Flagpole

Mizzen mast

Main yard

Barber-surgeon's cabin

Anti-boarding netting

Bow made of yew wood

Archer with quiver of arrows

Soldiers and archers

There were soldiers and archers on board, ready for any close-up fighting. Longbows, arrows, swords, and daggers were found by divers excavating the wreck. Netting stretched over the decks stopped enemies from climbing on board, but trapped the crew when the ship sank.

Bonaventure mizzen mast

English flag

Bulwarks

Sterncastle

The fatal day

On the day of the sinking the crew on board may have hoisted the sails wrongly. As the ship turned, the badly hoisted sails made her heel (roll) too much. Soldiers and guns tumbled towards the starboard side, turning the ship over even more until she filled with water and sank.

Bronze carriage gun

Transom

Sternpost

Barrels of tar

Hold

Spare blocks and rigging

Keelson

Keel made of elm

Gudgeon

Rudder

Pintle

TECHNICAL DATA

LENGTH (KEEL): 32 M (105 FT)

ARMAMENT:
15 BRONZE GUNS
76 IRON GUNS

WIDTH (BEAM): 11.4 M (37 FT 5 IN)

HULL MADE OF OAK

9

MAYFLOWER

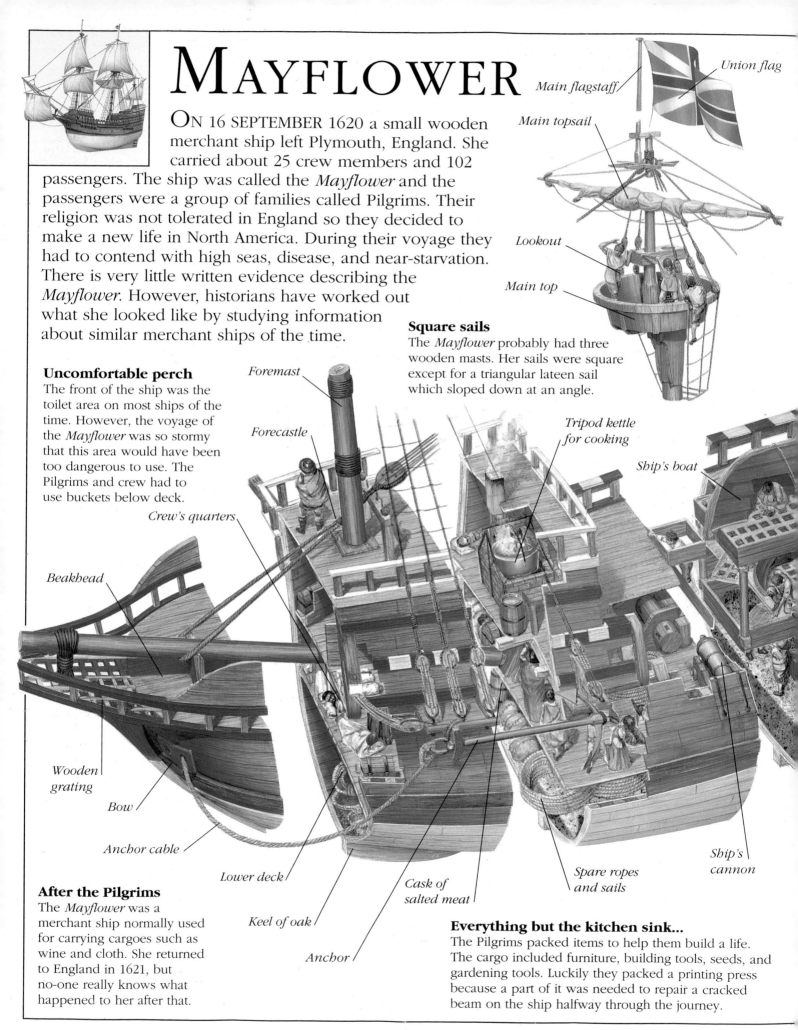

On 16 SEPTEMBER 1620 a small wooden merchant ship left Plymouth, England. She carried about 25 crew members and 102 passengers. The ship was called the *Mayflower* and the passengers were a group of families called Pilgrims. Their religion was not tolerated in England so they decided to make a new life in North America. During their voyage they had to contend with high seas, disease, and near-starvation. There is very little written evidence describing the *Mayflower*. However, historians have worked out what she looked like by studying information about similar merchant ships of the time.

Main flagstaff

Union flag

Main topsail

Lookout

Main top

Square sails
The *Mayflower* probably had three wooden masts. Her sails were square except for a triangular lateen sail which sloped down at an angle.

Uncomfortable perch
The front of the ship was the toilet area on most ships of the time. However, the voyage of the *Mayflower* was so stormy that this area would have been too dangerous to use. The Pilgrims and crew had to use buckets below deck.

Foremast

Forecastle

Crew's quarters

Tripod kettle for cooking

Ship's boat

Beakhead

Wooden grating

Bow

Anchor cable

Lower deck

Keel of oak

Anchor

Cask of salted meat

Spare ropes and sails

Ship's cannon

After the Pilgrims
The *Mayflower* was a merchant ship normally used for carrying cargoes such as wine and cloth. She returned to England in 1621, but no-one really knows what happened to her after that.

Everything but the kitchen sink...
The Pilgrims packed items to help them build a life. The cargo included furniture, building tools, seeds, and gardening tools. Luckily they packed a printing press because a part of it was needed to repair a cracked beam on the ship halfway through the journey.

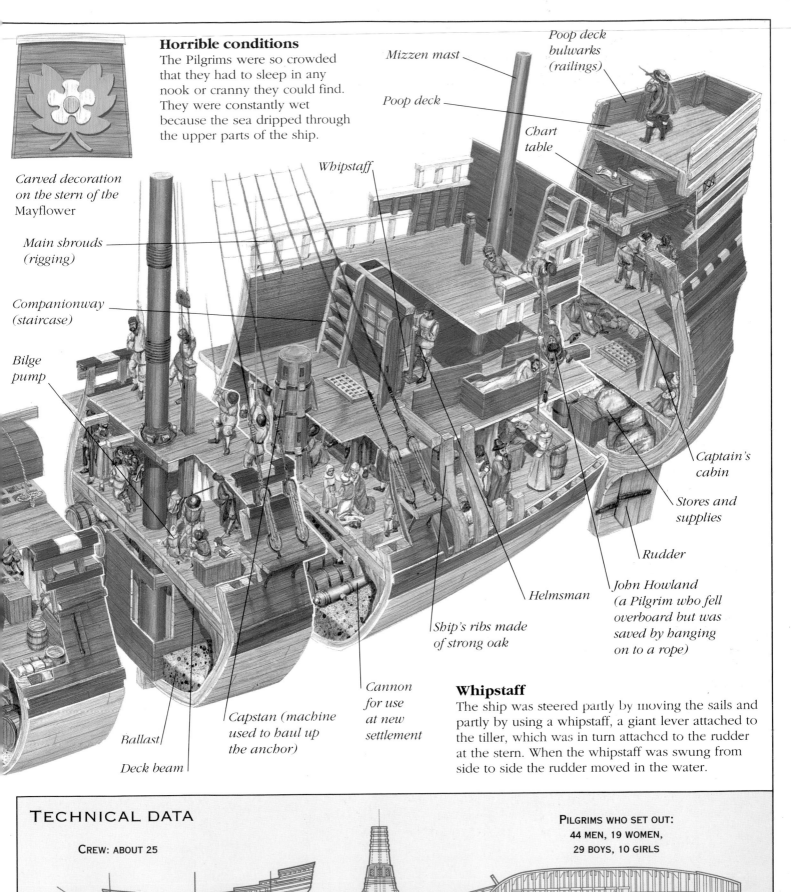

Horrible conditions
The Pilgrims were so crowded that they had to sleep in any nook or cranny they could find. They were constantly wet because the sea dripped through the upper parts of the ship.

Poop deck bulwarks (railings)

Mizzen mast

Poop deck

Chart table

Whipstaff

Carved decoration on the stern of the Mayflower

Main shrouds (rigging)

Companionway (staircase)

Bilge pump

Captain's cabin

Stores and supplies

Rudder

John Howland (a Pilgrim who fell overboard but was saved by hanging on to a rope)

Helmsman

Ship's ribs made of strong oak

Ballast

Deck beam

Capstan (machine used to haul up the anchor)

Cannon for use at new settlement

Whipstaff
The ship was steered partly by moving the sails and partly by using a whipstaff, a giant lever attached to the tiller, which was in turn attached to the rudder at the stern. When the whipstaff was swung from side to side the rudder moved in the water.

TECHNICAL DATA

CREW: ABOUT 25

PILGRIMS WHO SET OUT:
44 MEN, 19 WOMEN,
29 BOYS, 10 GIRLS

HEIGHT (MAINMAST): 29.5 M (97 FT)

WIDTH (BEAM): 8 M (26 FT)

APPROX LENGTH: 29 M (95 FT 6 IN)

HMS PANDORA

IN 1790 HMS *PANDORA* set sail from England. Her mission was to catch the most notorious mutineers in naval history. Her story began with the voyage of another ship, HMS *Bounty*. In 1787 the *Bounty* sailed to Tahiti in the Pacific. It seemed a paradise to the disgruntled British crewmen and they mutinied rather than return home. On her later voyage, the *Pandora* captured fourteen mutineers, but then hit the Great Barrier Reef off North Queensland, Australia, and sank. In 1977 the wreck was found and since then the contents have been carefully excavated.

Ship's boats

Boat support cradle

Foremast

Belfry

Galley chimney

Bowsprit

Swivel gun

Fo'c'sle deck

Cathead

Decks

The *Pandora* had a lower deck and a main deck, which was partly open to the sky. At either end of the ship there were raised decks, the fo'c'sle forward and the quarterdeck aft. Crewmen were crowded into the forward parts of the ship. Supplies were stored in the hold at the bottom of the ship.

Figurehead

Anchor

Figurehead

Like other warships of her day, *Pandora* carried a figurehead on her bow. The figure represents Pandora, the character from Greek mythology.

Attaching dowels

Cutwater

Copper-plated bottom

Carved wooden drapery

Galley stove

Swift ship

HMS *Pandora* was a type of warship called a frigate. This meant she had fewer than 50 guns. Frigates were small and fast. They did scouting duties rather than joining in big battles.

Hold

Mainmast

Capstan

Ship's
wheel

"Pandora's
box" cell

Captain's
great cabin

Main
deck

9-pounder
gun

Sailor's hammock

Spare ropes
and cables

Gunpowder magazine
(storage room)

Casks of fresh
water and
salted meat

LENGTH:	WIDTH (BEAM):
120 FT	9.75 M
(36.5 M)	(32 FT)

CREW:	PANDORA'S BOX:
UNKNOWN	LENGTH ON DECK
	3.4 M (11 FT),
	WIDTH
	5.5 M (18 FT)

ARMAMENT:	
22 9-POUNDERS	6 18-POUNDER
2 3-POUNDERS	CARRONADES

"Smasher" guns

There were 24 main guns on board.
Some of them were a new type called
carronades. They were nicknamed
"smashers" because they could fire big
cannonballs that did a lot of damage
at short range. They could also fire
grapeshot, bags of small cannonballs
that killed crew members.

An officer's life for me

The officers lived in the stern of
the ship where they had light,
airy cabins with glass windows.
The captain's great cabin was the
most luxurious. It even had an
ornate fireplace, later recovered
from the wreck.

Loader

Gunner

18-pounder
carronade

Ammunition

Ropes and
blocks to
move gun

Pandora's box

A wooden cell was built on the poop
deck for the prisoners. When the ship
began to sink they all managed to escape
except for one man who was drowned
still in his leg-irons. Another three
drowned in the sea.

BATTLESHIP

IN THE LATE NINETEENTH CENTURY marine steam power was improved, and cannonballs were replaced by exploding shells. Soon tall-masted warships were a thing of the past. They were replaced by new battleships with hulls built first of iron and then, later on, of steel. The greatest change came in 1906 when HMS *Dreadnought* was launched at Portsmouth, England. Her designers had included so many new ideas that she made every other existing battleship look old-fashioned and useless! Her steam turbine engines made her faster. Her big guns were larger and more accurate than any seen before. She was the first of a new generation of ships that changed the way sea-battles were fought.

Searchlight platform

Foretop

Tripod foremast

Forward funnel

Navigation bridge

Wheelhouse

Searchlight

Conning tower

A turret

12-inch gun

Armoured barbette

Torpedo catchers
Giant nets could be hung over the side to catch torpedoes fired from enemy submarines. If a torpedo did slip through, thick steel armour plating stopped it from blasting a hole in the hull.

Forepeak

Main anchor

Provision room

Meat room

Torpedo tube

Torpedo

Anti-torpedo nets

Admiral's dining cabin

Coal bunkers

Galley

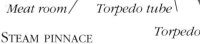

STEAM PINNACE

Funnel

Wheel

Cabin

Ship's boats
The ship carried several small boats, like the steam-powered pinnace shown here. They were used to ferry officers and supplies to and from shore.

Full steam ahead!
The *Dreadnought*'s turbine engines were fast and reliable. Inside them, steam pushed against thousands of blades mounted on shafts that spun around, driving the ship's propellers.

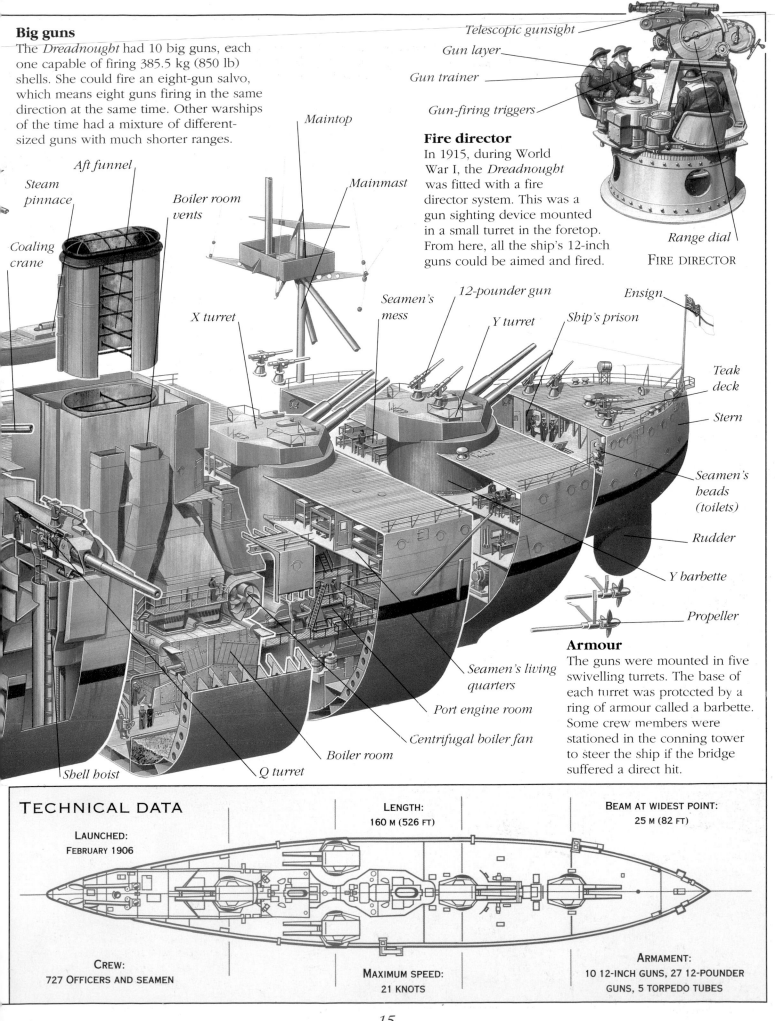

Big guns

The *Dreadnought* had 10 big guns, each one capable of firing 385.5 kg (850 lb) shells. She could fire an eight-gun salvo, which means eight guns firing in the same direction at the same time. Other warships of the time had a mixture of different-sized guns with much shorter ranges.

Telescopic gunsight

Gun layer

Gun trainer

Gun-firing triggers

Fire director

In 1915, during World War I, the *Dreadnought* was fitted with a fire director system. This was a gun sighting device mounted in a small turret in the foretop. From here, all the ship's 12-inch guns could be aimed and fired.

Range dial

FIRE DIRECTOR

Maintop

Aft funnel

Steam pinnace

Boiler room vents

Coaling crane

Mainmast

X turret

Seamen's mess

12-pounder gun

Y turret

Ensign

Ship's prison

Teak deck

Stern

Seamen's heads (toilets)

Rudder

Y barbette

Propeller

Seamen's living quarters

Port engine room

Centrifugal boiler fan

Boiler room

Shell hoist

Q turret

Armour

The guns were mounted in five swivelling turrets. The base of each turret was protected by a ring of armour called a barbette. Some crew members were stationed in the conning tower to steer the ship if the bridge suffered a direct hit.

TECHNICAL DATA

LAUNCHED:
FEBRUARY 1906

LENGTH:
160 M (526 FT)

BEAM AT WIDEST POINT:
25 M (82 FT)

CREW:
727 OFFICERS AND SEAMEN

MAXIMUM SPEED:
21 KNOTS

ARMAMENT:
10 12-INCH GUNS, 27 12-POUNDER GUNS, 5 TORPEDO TUBES

CANBERRA

A MODERN OCEAN LINER is more than just a sailing ship. It is a huge floating hotel with lots of luxuries onboard. The passengers can sunbathe on deck, take a dip in a swimming pool, play sports, go shopping, or watch a movie. The most important job for the crew is to make sure that everyone has a comfortable and relaxing time. This picture shows the *Canberra*. Launched in 1960, she is still used for cruises today. When she was built she was hailed as the shape of things to come. Her sleek elegant hull and below-deck layout have since been copied on ocean liners all over the world.

Twin funnels

Life of luxury
Most of the passenger cabins are in the middle part of the ship, far away from any noise or vibration made by the engines. In between the cabin areas there are lounges, shops, hairdressers, libraries, and playrooms for young children.

Red Ensign

Games deck

Nested lifeboat

Swimming pool

Bridge wing

Radar scanner

Stern

Rudder

Starboard propeller

Tourist-class accommodation

Boiler room

Engine room

First-class accommodation

Welded steel hull

Smooth ride
The *Canberra* is a high-speed ship. Her hull is shaped so that it slips easily through the water. Above the waterline everything is kept as smooth and rounded as possible. The lifeboats are "nested", which means they are fitted into recesses along the sides.

Stabilizer

Galley

Drink store

CANBERRA'S PROPELLERS

Refrigerating machinery

Full speed ahead!
The two propellers are situated at the stern of the ship, on either side of the hull. They push the *Canberra* forwards through the water at an average speed of 27.5 knots.

Powerful engines
Unlike most previous liners the engines are near the stern. Steam-driven turbines are used to create electricity to run motors. These turn the two propellers underneath the stern. The ship uses 4.5 litres (1 gallon) of fuel to travel 16 m (53 ft).

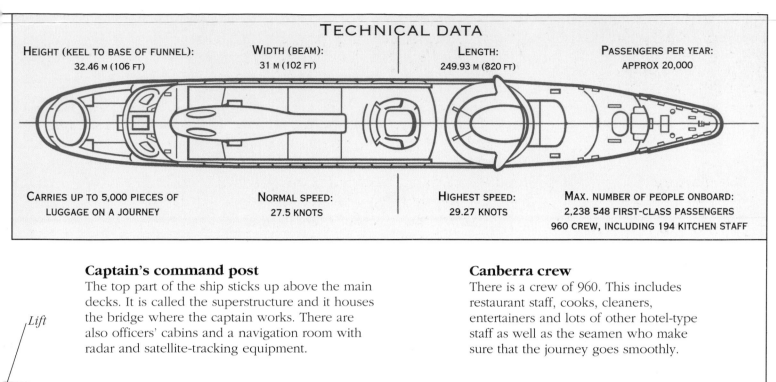

TECHNICAL DATA

HEIGHT (KEEL TO BASE OF FUNNEL): 32.46 M (106 FT)	WIDTH (BEAM): 31 M (102 FT)	LENGTH: 249.93 M (820 FT)	PASSENGERS PER YEAR: APPROX 20,000
CARRIES UP TO 5,000 PIECES OF LUGGAGE ON A JOURNEY	NORMAL SPEED: 27.5 KNOTS	HIGHEST SPEED: 29.27 KNOTS	MAX. NUMBER OF PEOPLE ONBOARD: 2,238 548 FIRST-CLASS PASSENGERS 960 CREW, INCLUDING 194 KITCHEN STAFF

Captain's command post

The top part of the ship sticks up above the main decks. It is called the superstructure and it houses the bridge where the captain works. There are also officers' cabins and a navigation room with radar and satellite-tracking equipment.

Canberra crew

There is a crew of 960. This includes restaurant staff, cooks, cleaners, entertainers and lots of other hotel-type staff as well as the seamen who make sure that the journey goes smoothly.

Food facts

It takes 90 days for the *Canberra* to complete a world cruise. During this time 675,000 main meals are prepared using, among other ingredients, 400,000 eggs. More than 250,000 cakes and pastries are baked, together with 35,000 loaves and half a million bread rolls!

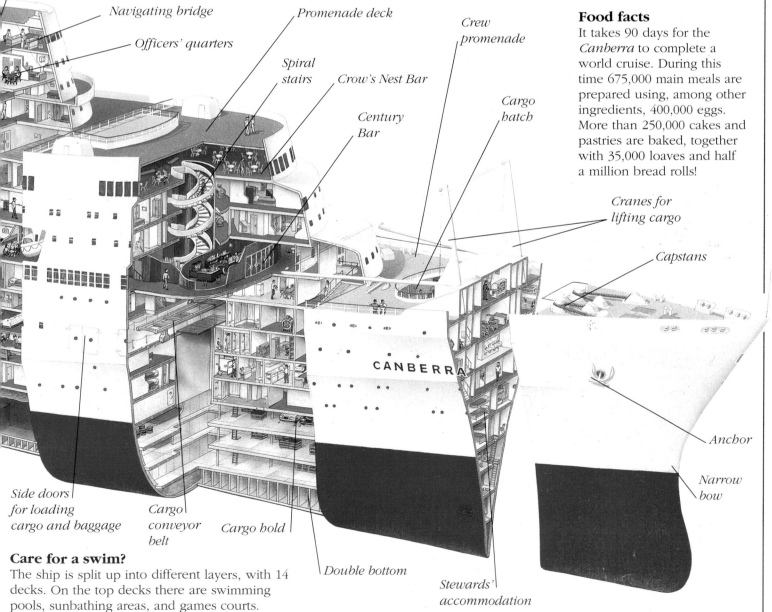

Lift

Navigating bridge

Officers' quarters

Promenade deck

Spiral stairs

Crow's Nest Bar

Century Bar

Crew promenade

Cargo hatch

Cranes for lifting cargo

Capstans

Anchor

Narrow bow

Side doors for loading cargo and baggage

Cargo conveyor belt

Cargo hold

Double bottom

Stewards' accommodation

Care for a swim?

The ship is split up into different layers, with 14 decks. On the top decks there are swimming pools, sunbathing areas, and games courts.

AIRCRAFT CARRIER

AIRCRAFT CARRIERS ARE THE WORLD'S biggest warships. Their giant steel hulls tower high above the waves and their flight decks stretch out for the length of the ship. A carrier does not need to get close to the enemy. Its aircraft can take off from the deck to bomb a target far away. During World War II, American Essex-class aircraft-carriers fought important battles in the Pacific Ocean. Many of their features are still on today's carriers. They carried over a hundred aeroplanes, thousands of crew members, and big stores of ammunition and fuel. This picture shows the USS *Lexington*, an Essex-class which served in the Pacific.

Kamikaze!
One of the main dangers to World War II carriers came from Japanese *Kamikaze* suicide planes. They were so packed with explosives that they became piloted bombs which the pilots tried to crash into enemy ships.

Up and away
When an aircraft took off from the ship it needed to get up speed quickly. It was attached by a hook to runners that slid along tracks on the flight deck. Powered by steam, the runners shot the aeroplane forward, the hook uncoupled, and the aircraft took off. This equipment was called a steam catapult.

BOFORS 40-MM AA GUNS
- Double barrel
- Elevation trunnion
- Flashguard
- Spent cartridge chutes
- Firing pedal
- Swivelling base

Shooting down the enemy
Carriers could be attacked by enemy planes so they were fitted with lots of small rapid-firing anti-aircraft ('AA') guns to shoot them down at close range. The crew wore white hoods to protect them from flash burns as they fired.

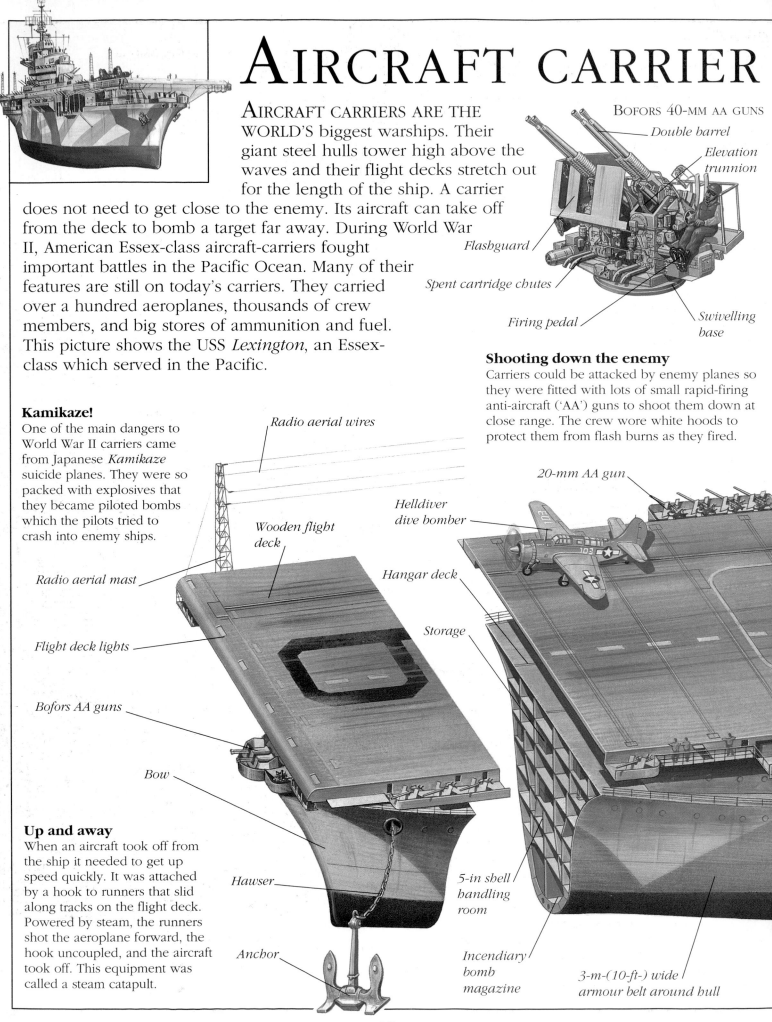

- Radio aerial wires
- Radio aerial mast
- Flight deck lights
- Bofors AA guns
- Bow
- Hawser
- Anchor
- Wooden flight deck
- 20-mm AA gun
- Helldiver dive bomber
- Hangar deck
- Storage
- 5-in shell handling room
- Incendiary bomb magazine
- 3-m-(10-ft-) wide armour belt around hull

On the island

The bridge, the funnel, and the navigation rooms were all above the flight deck in a structure called the "island". It was built to one side so that the flight deck was kept clear. On top there was radio and radar equipment, including fire directors.

Seagoing aeroplanes

There was room for over a hundred aircraft on board, including fighters, dive-bombers, fighter-bombers, and torpedo bombers. Each type of plane carried out a different form of attack. They were all fitted with wings that could fold up for easy storage.

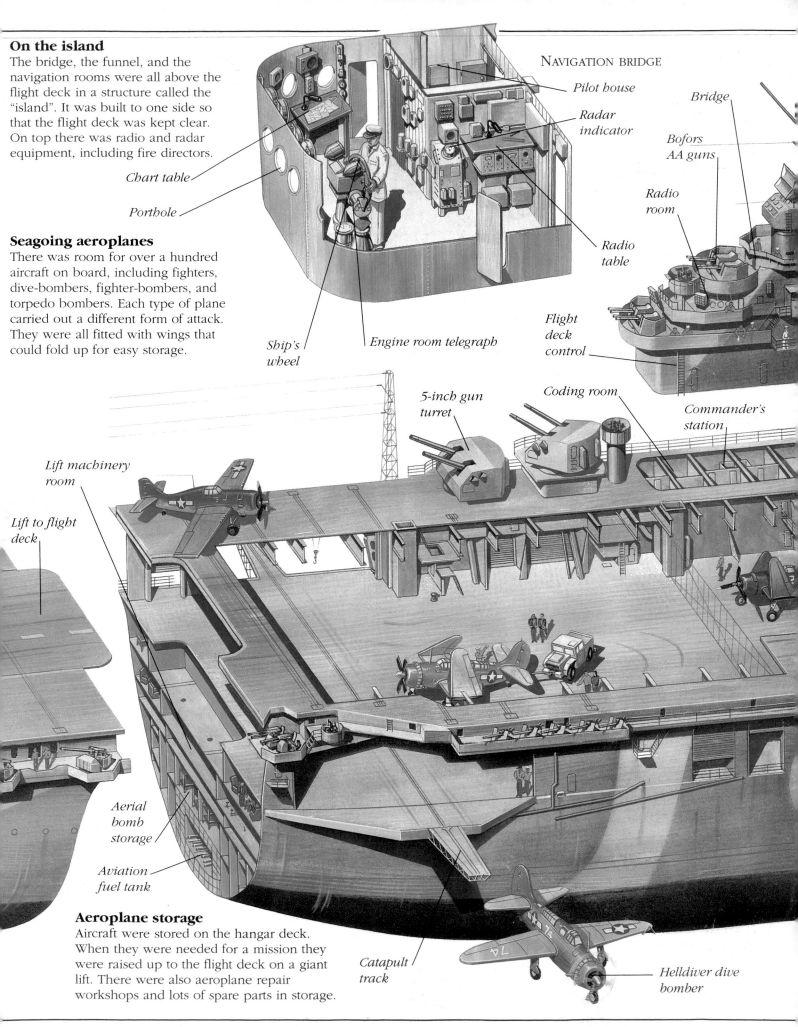

NAVIGATION BRIDGE

Pilot house

Radar indicator

Radio table

Bridge

Bofors AA guns

Radio room

Flight deck control

Chart table

Porthole

Ship's wheel

Engine room telegraph

Coding room

Commander's station

5-inch gun turret

Lift machinery room

Lift to flight deck

Aerial bomb storage

Aviation fuel tank

Catapult track

Helldiver dive bomber

Aeroplane storage

Aircraft were stored on the hangar deck. When they were needed for a mission they were raised up to the flight deck on a giant lift. There were also aeroplane repair workshops and lots of spare parts in storage.

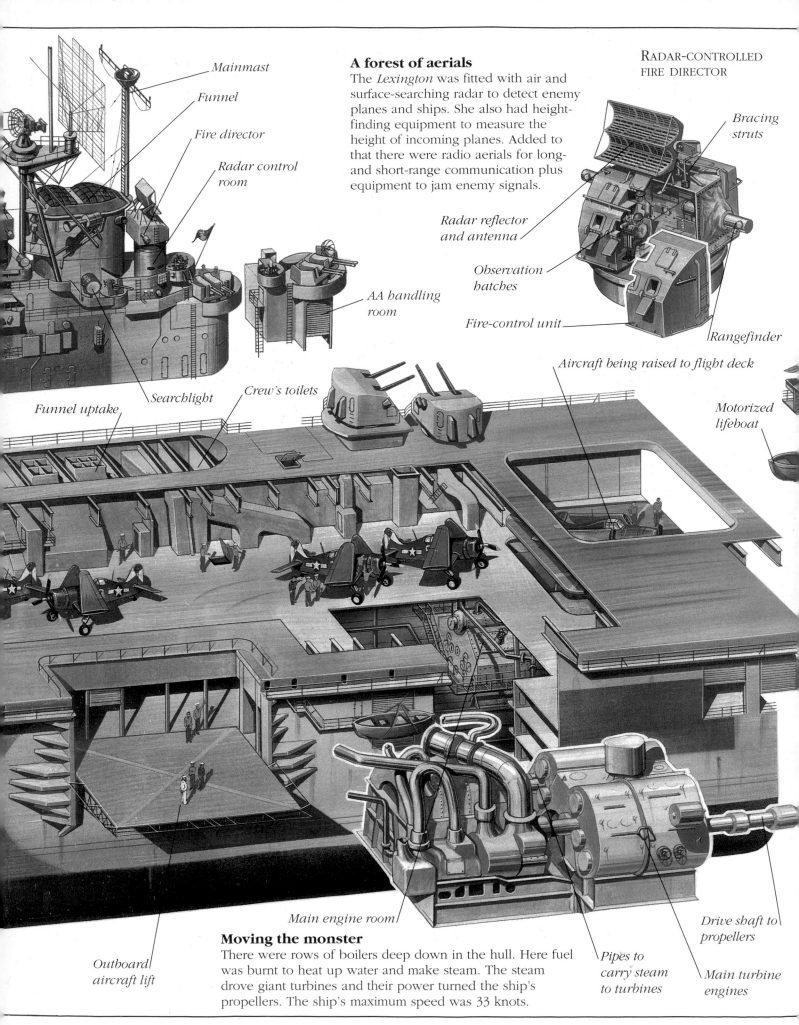

Mainmast

Funnel

Fire director

Radar control room

A forest of aerials

The *Lexington* was fitted with air and surface-searching radar to detect enemy planes and ships. She also had height-finding equipment to measure the height of incoming planes. Added to that there were radio aerials for long- and short-range communication plus equipment to jam enemy signals.

RADAR-CONTROLLED FIRE DIRECTOR

Bracing struts

Radar reflector and antenna

Observation hatches

Fire-control unit

Rangefinder

AA handling room

Funnel uptake

Searchlight

Crew's toilets

Aircraft being raised to flight deck

Motorized lifeboat

Outboard aircraft lift

Main engine room

Moving the monster

There were rows of boilers deep down in the hull. Here fuel was burnt to heat up water and make steam. The steam drove giant turbines and their power turned the ship's propellers. The ship's maximum speed was 33 knots.

Pipes to carry steam to turbines

Drive shaft to propellers

Main turbine engines

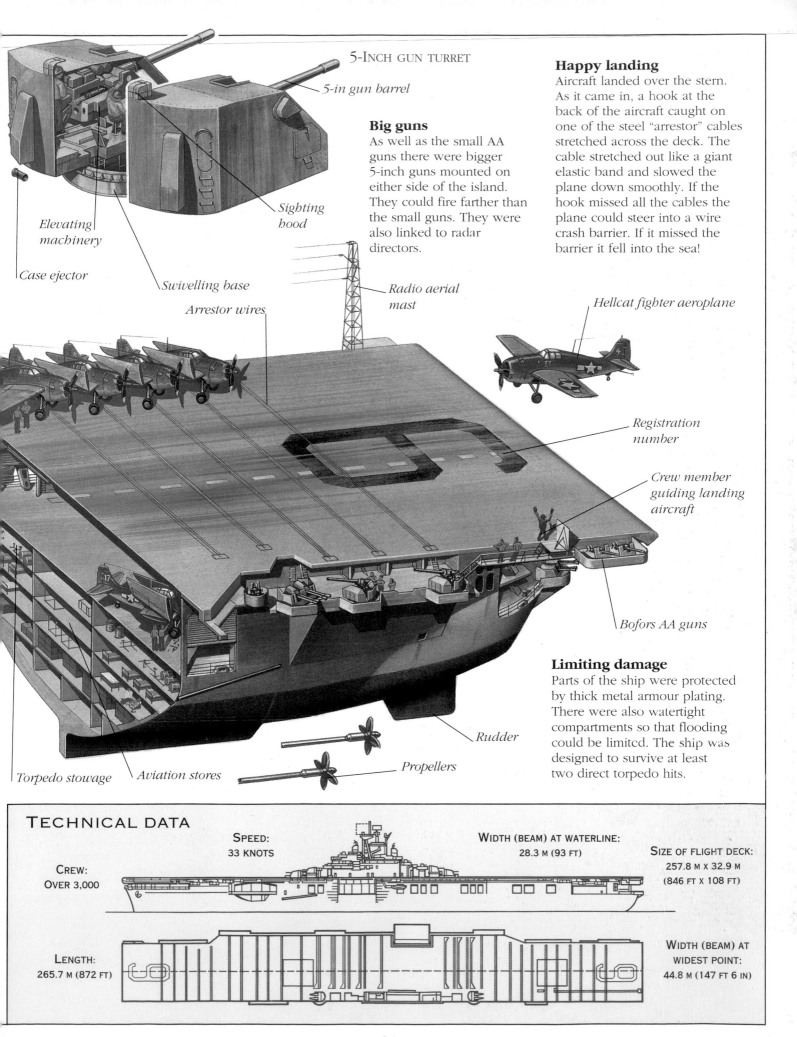

5-INCH GUN TURRET

5-in gun barrel

Sighting hood

Elevating machinery

Case ejector

Swivelling base

Big guns

As well as the small AA guns there were bigger 5-inch guns mounted on either side of the island. They could fire farther than the small guns. They were also linked to radar directors.

Happy landing

Aircraft landed over the stern. As it came in, a hook at the back of the aircraft caught on one of the steel "arrestor" cables stretched across the deck. The cable stretched out like a giant elastic band and slowed the plane down smoothly. If the hook missed all the cables the plane could steer into a wire crash barrier. If it missed the barrier it fell into the sea!

Arrestor wires

Radio aerial mast

Hellcat fighter aeroplane

Registration number

Crew member guiding landing aircraft

Bofors AA guns

Limiting damage

Parts of the ship were protected by thick metal armour plating. There were also watertight compartments so that flooding could be limited. The ship was designed to survive at least two direct torpedo hits.

Rudder

Propellers

Torpedo stowage

Aviation stores

TECHNICAL DATA

CREW: OVER 3,000

SPEED: 33 KNOTS

WIDTH (BEAM) AT WATERLINE: 28.3 M (93 FT)

SIZE OF FLIGHT DECK: 257.8 M X 32.9 M (846 FT X 108 FT)

LENGTH: 265.7 M (872 FT)

WIDTH (BEAM) AT WIDEST POINT: 44.8 M (147 FT 6 IN)

CHINESE JUNK

IN THE THIRTEENTH CENTURY a Venetian called Marco Polo became one of the first travellers ever to reach China. He marvelled at the many sights, including strange, brightly painted boats. In some ways these boats were far in advance of anything the Europeans could build at that time. For instance, they had a rudder fitted at the back of the stern and watertight compartments below deck. These boats still exist today, and are called junks. For hundreds of years they have sailed up rivers and along the coast. There are many different types of junks. This is a seagoing version from the Foochow region of China.

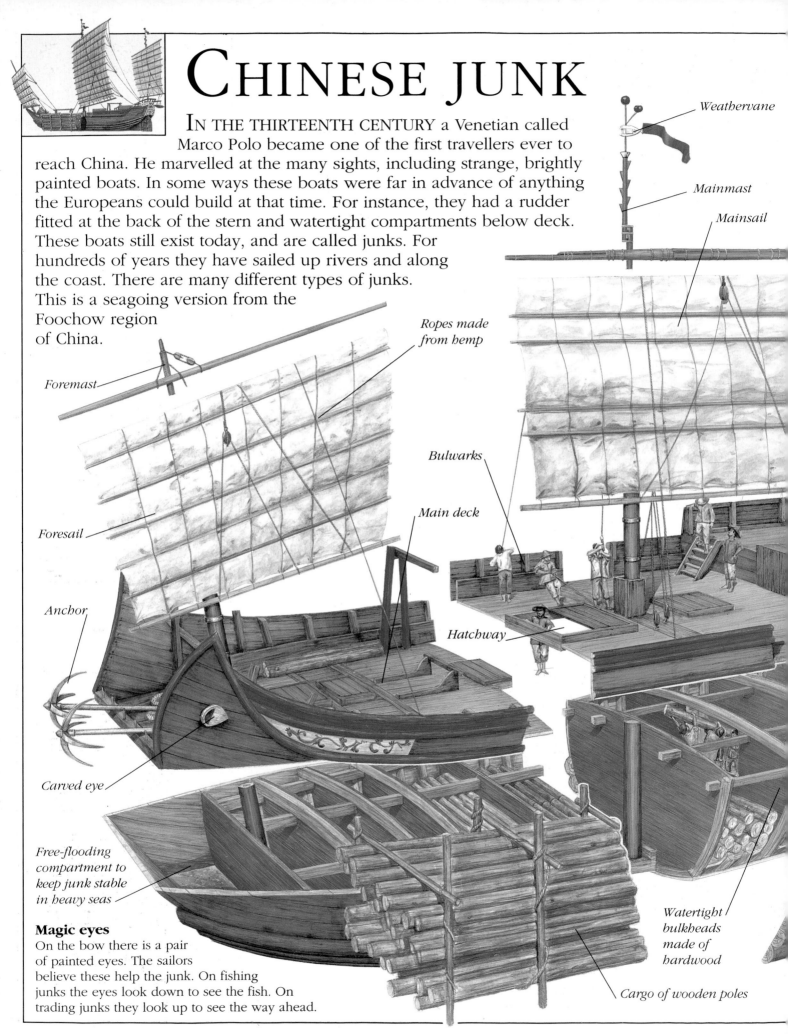

Weathervane

Mainmast

Mainsail

Ropes made from hemp

Foremast

Bulwarks

Main deck

Foresail

Anchor

Hatchway

Carved eye

Free-flooding compartment to keep junk stable in heavy seas

Watertight bulkheads made of hardwood

Cargo of wooden poles

Magic eyes
On the bow there is a pair of painted eyes. The sailors believe these help the junk. On fishing junks the eyes look down to see the fish. On trading junks they look up to see the way ahead.

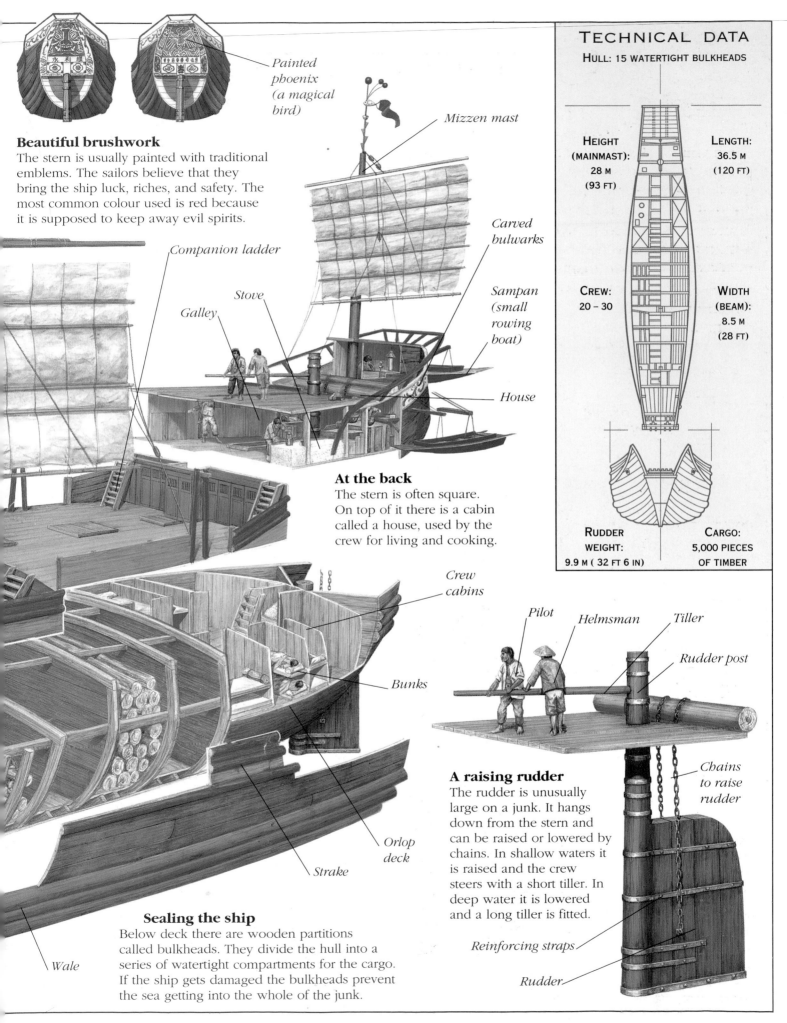

Painted phoenix (a magical bird)

Beautiful brushwork

The stern is usually painted with traditional emblems. The sailors believe that they bring the ship luck, riches, and safety. The most common colour used is red because it is supposed to keep away evil spirits.

Mizzen mast

Companion ladder

Stove

Galley

Carved bulwarks

Sampan (small rowing boat)

House

At the back

The stern is often square. On top of it there is a cabin called a house, used by the crew for living and cooking.

TECHNICAL DATA
HULL: 15 WATERTIGHT BULKHEADS

HEIGHT (MAINMAST): 28 M (93 FT)	**LENGTH:** 36.5 M (120 FT)
CREW: 20 – 30	**WIDTH (BEAM):** 8.5 M (28 FT)
RUDDER WEIGHT: 9.9 M (32 FT 6 IN)	**CARGO:** 5,000 PIECES OF TIMBER

Crew cabins

Bunks

Pilot *Helmsman* *Tiller*

Rudder post

Chains to raise rudder

A raising rudder

The rudder is unusually large on a junk. It hangs down from the stern and can be raised or lowered by chains. In shallow waters it is raised and the crew steers with a short tiller. In deep water it is lowered and a long tiller is fitted.

Orlop deck

Strake

Wale

Sealing the ship

Below deck there are wooden partitions called bulkheads. They divide the hull into a series of watertight compartments for the cargo. If the ship gets damaged the bulkheads prevent the sea getting into the whole of the junk.

Reinforcing straps

Rudder

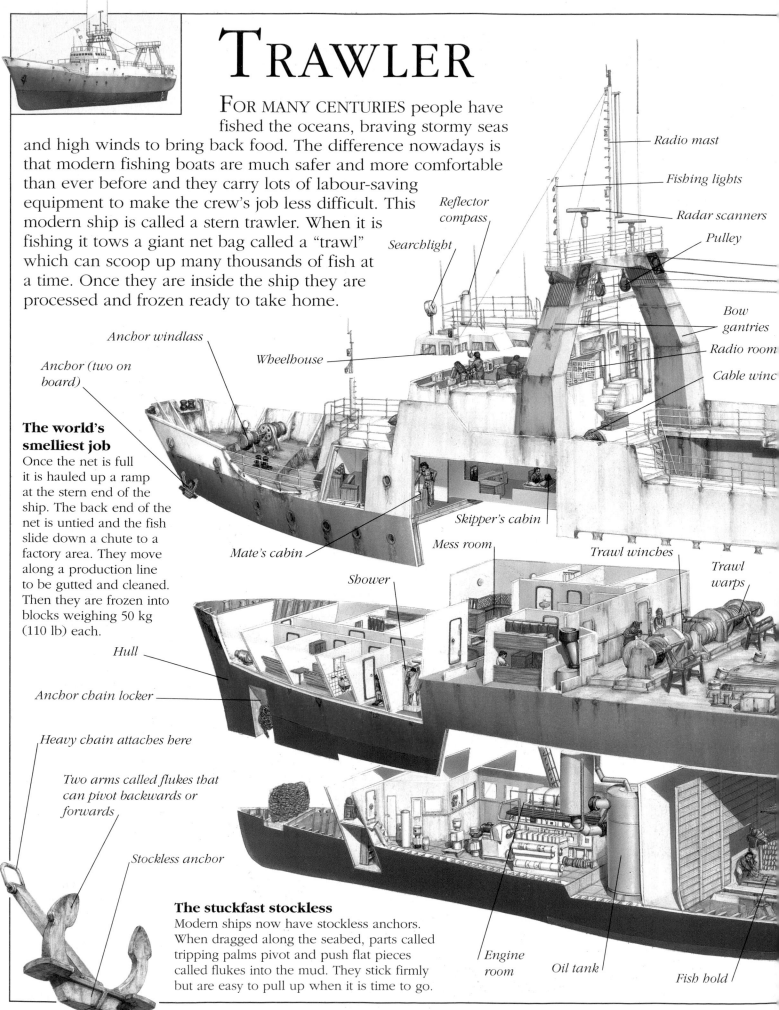

TRAWLER

FOR MANY CENTURIES people have fished the oceans, braving stormy seas and high winds to bring back food. The difference nowadays is that modern fishing boats are much safer and more comfortable than ever before and they carry lots of labour-saving equipment to make the crew's job less difficult. This modern ship is called a stern trawler. When it is fishing it tows a giant net bag called a "trawl" which can scoop up many thousands of fish at a time. Once they are inside the ship they are processed and frozen ready to take home.

Radio mast

Fishing lights

Radar scanners

Reflector compass

Pulley

Searchlight

Bow gantries

Anchor windlass

Radio room

Wheelhouse

Cable winc

Anchor (two on board)

The world's smelliest job
Once the net is full it is hauled up a ramp at the stern end of the ship. The back end of the net is untied and the fish slide down a chute to a factory area. They move along a production line to be gutted and cleaned. Then they are frozen into blocks weighing 50 kg (110 lb) each.

Skipper's cabin

Mate's cabin

Mess room

Trawl winches

Shower

Trawl warps

Hull

Anchor chain locker

Heavy chain attaches here

Two arms called flukes that can pivot backwards or forwards

Stockless anchor

The stuckfast stockless
Modern ships now have stockless anchors. When dragged along the seabed, parts called tripping palms pivot and push flat pieces called flukes into the mud. They stick firmly but are easy to pull up when it is time to go.

Engine room

Oil tank

Fish hold

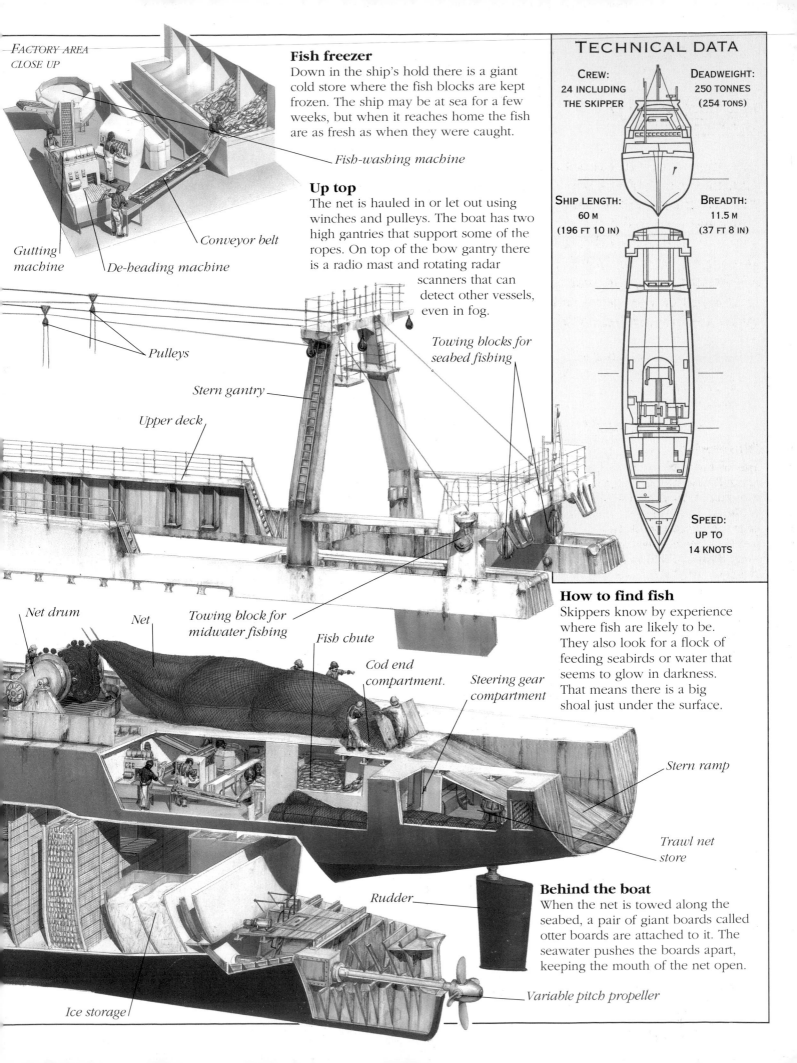

FACTORY AREA CLOSE UP

Fish freezer
Down in the ship's hold there is a giant cold store where the fish blocks are kept frozen. The ship may be at sea for a few weeks, but when it reaches home the fish are as fresh as when they were caught.

Fish-washing machine

Gutting machine

De-heading machine

Conveyor belt

Up top
The net is hauled in or let out using winches and pulleys. The boat has two high gantries that support some of the ropes. On top of the bow gantry there is a radio mast and rotating radar scanners that can detect other vessels, even in fog.

Pulleys

Stern gantry

Towing blocks for seabed fishing

Upper deck

Net drum

Net

Towing block for midwater fishing

Fish chute

Cod end compartment.

Steering gear compartment

Ice storage

Rudder

Stern ramp

Trawl net store

Variable pitch propeller

TECHNICAL DATA

CREW:
24 INCLUDING THE SKIPPER

DEADWEIGHT:
250 TONNES
(254 TONS)

SHIP LENGTH:
60 M
(196 FT 10 IN)

BREADTH:
11.5 M
(37 FT 8 IN)

SPEED:
UP TO
14 KNOTS

How to find fish
Skippers know by experience where fish are likely to be. They also look for a flock of feeding seabirds or water that seems to glow in darkness. That means there is a big shoal just under the surface.

Behind the boat
When the net is towed along the seabed, a pair of giant boards called otter boards are attached to it. The seawater pushes the boards apart, keeping the mouth of the net open.

LIFEBOAT

NEXT TIME YOU WATCH A STORM from your window, imagine what it would be like to be at sea off the rugged rocky coast of Britain, with wind whipping the waves and rain lashing into your face. That's just the kind of weather in which a boat might get into trouble and an RNLI lifeboat would be called to the rescue. The RNLI is the world's oldest lifeboat service, with stations all around the British coast. The lifeboat shown here is an RNLI Tyne Class. Crew members are all volunteers. Once the lifeboat is called out they get to the lifeboat station as fast as they can. As soon as they are on board the boat runs down a slipway, hits the water with a mighty splash, and races off to the rescue site.

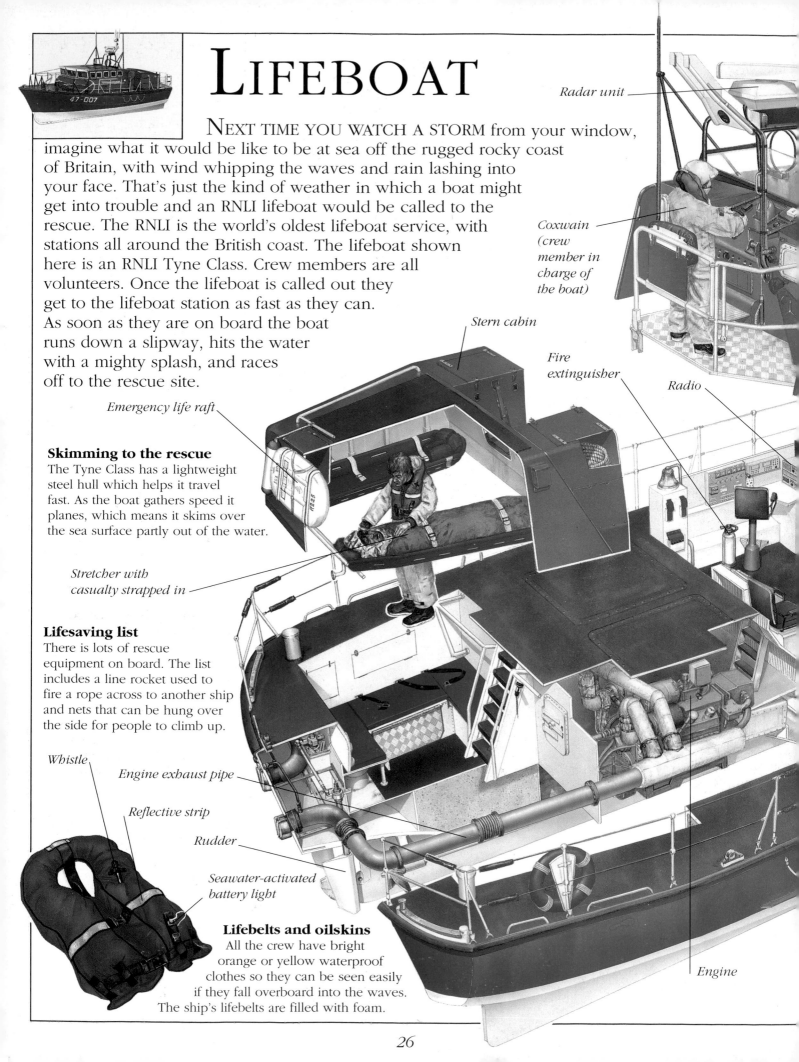

Radar unit

Coxwain (crew member in charge of the boat)

Stern cabin

Fire extinguisher

Radio

Emergency life raft

Skimming to the rescue
The Tyne Class has a lightweight steel hull which helps it travel fast. As the boat gathers speed it planes, which means it skims over the sea surface partly out of the water.

Stretcher with casualty strapped in

Lifesaving list
There is lots of rescue equipment on board. The list includes a line rocket used to fire a rope across to another ship and nets that can be hung over the side for people to climb up.

Whistle

Engine exhaust pipe

Reflective strip

Rudder

Seawater-activated battery light

Lifebelts and oilskins
All the crew have bright orange or yellow waterproof clothes so they can be seen easily if they fall overboard into the waves. The ship's lifebelts are filled with foam.

Engine

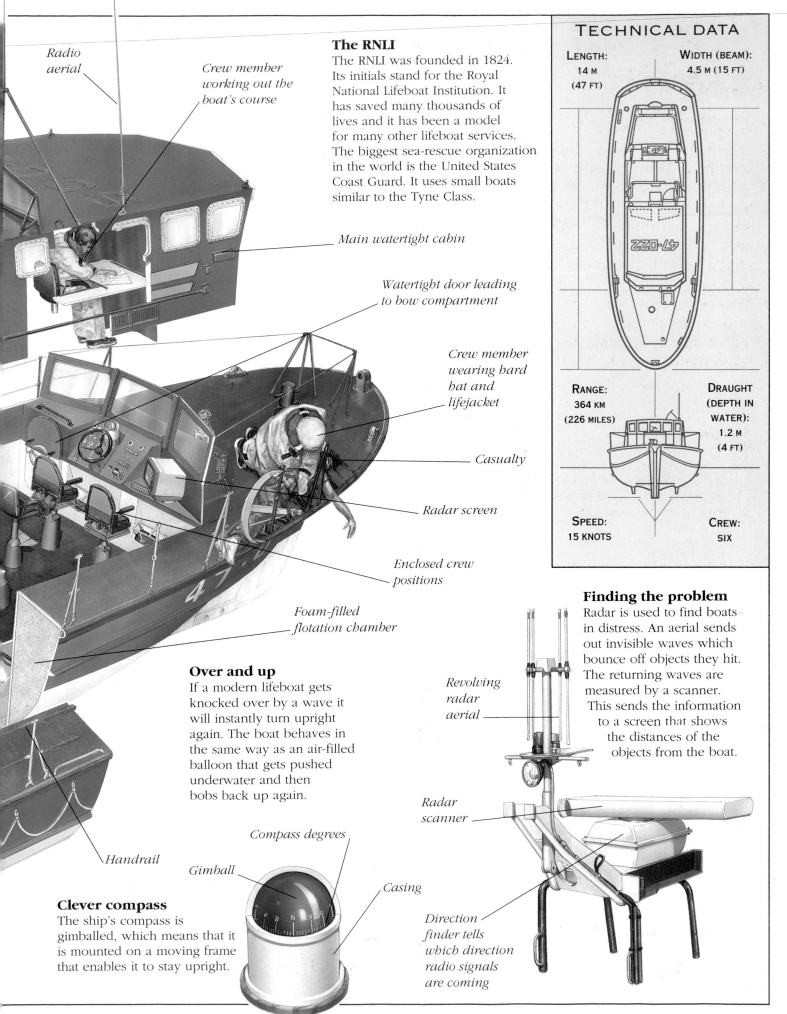

Radio aerial

Crew member working out the boat's course

The RNLI
The RNLI was founded in 1824. Its initials stand for the Royal National Lifeboat Institution. It has saved many thousands of lives and it has been a model for many other lifeboat services. The biggest sea-rescue organization in the world is the United States Coast Guard. It uses small boats similar to the Tyne Class.

Main watertight cabin

Watertight door leading to bow compartment

Crew member wearing hard hat and lifejacket

Casualty

Radar screen

Enclosed crew positions

Foam-filled flotation chamber

Over and up
If a modern lifeboat gets knocked over by a wave it will instantly turn upright again. The boat behaves in the same way as an air-filled balloon that gets pushed underwater and then bobs back up again.

Handrail

Compass degrees

Gimball

Casing

Clever compass
The ship's compass is gimballed, which means that it is mounted on a moving frame that enables it to stay upright.

TECHNICAL DATA

LENGTH: 14 M (47 FT)	WIDTH (BEAM): 4.5 M (15 FT)

RANGE: 364 KM (226 MILES)	DRAUGHT (DEPTH IN WATER): 1.2 M (4 FT)

SPEED: 15 KNOTS	CREW: SIX

Finding the problem
Radar is used to find boats in distress. An aerial sends out invisible waves which bounce off objects they hit. The returning waves are measured by a scanner. This sends the information to a screen that shows the distances of the objects from the boat.

Revolving radar aerial

Radar scanner

Direction finder tells which direction radio signals are coming

NAUTICAL TIMELINE

THE HISTORY of ships stretches back
thousands of years. The first boats were
made from inflated skins, hollowed-out
logs, or bundles of reeds tied together.
Over the centuries since that time ship
design has gradually changed and it is still
changing today. Here are some milestones
in the development of the modern vessel.

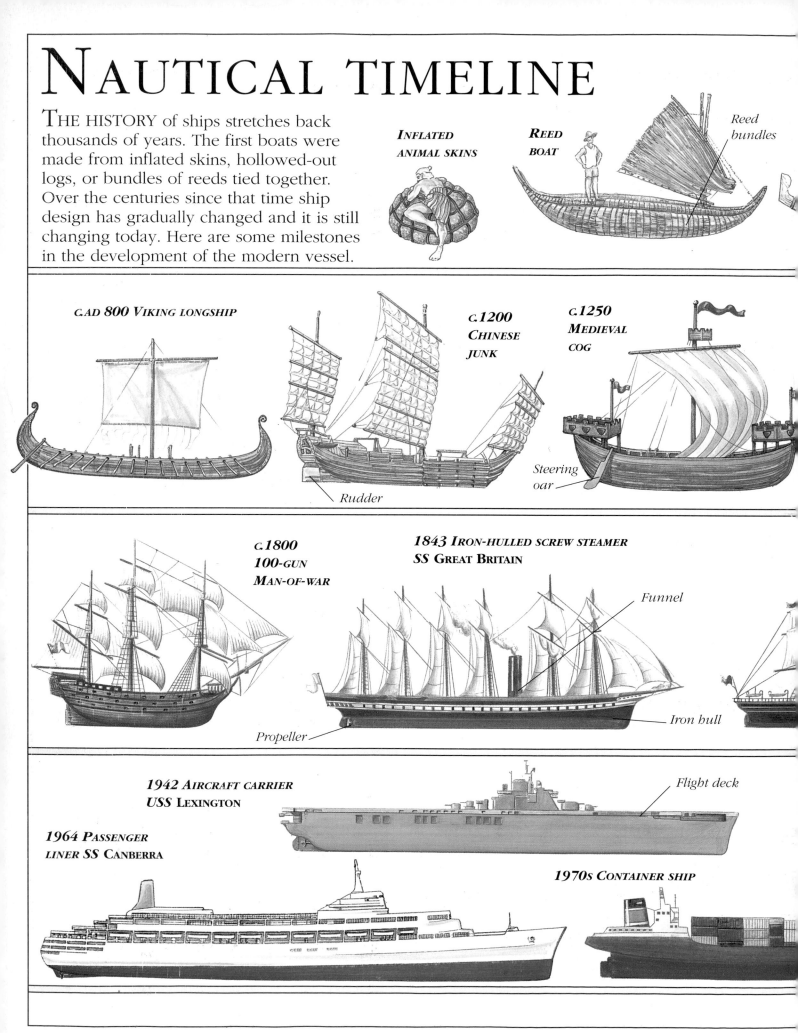

**INFLATED
ANIMAL SKINS**

**REED
BOAT**

Reed
bundles

c.AD 800 VIKING LONGSHIP

*c.1200
CHINESE
JUNK*

*c.1250
MEDIEVAL
COG*

Steering
oar

Rudder

*c.1800
100-GUN
MAN-OF-WAR*

*1843 IRON-HULLED SCREW STEAMER
SS GREAT BRITAIN*

Funnel

Iron hull

Propeller

*1942 AIRCRAFT CARRIER
USS LEXINGTON*

Flight deck

*1964 PASSENGER
LINER SS CANBERRA*

1970s CONTAINER SHIP

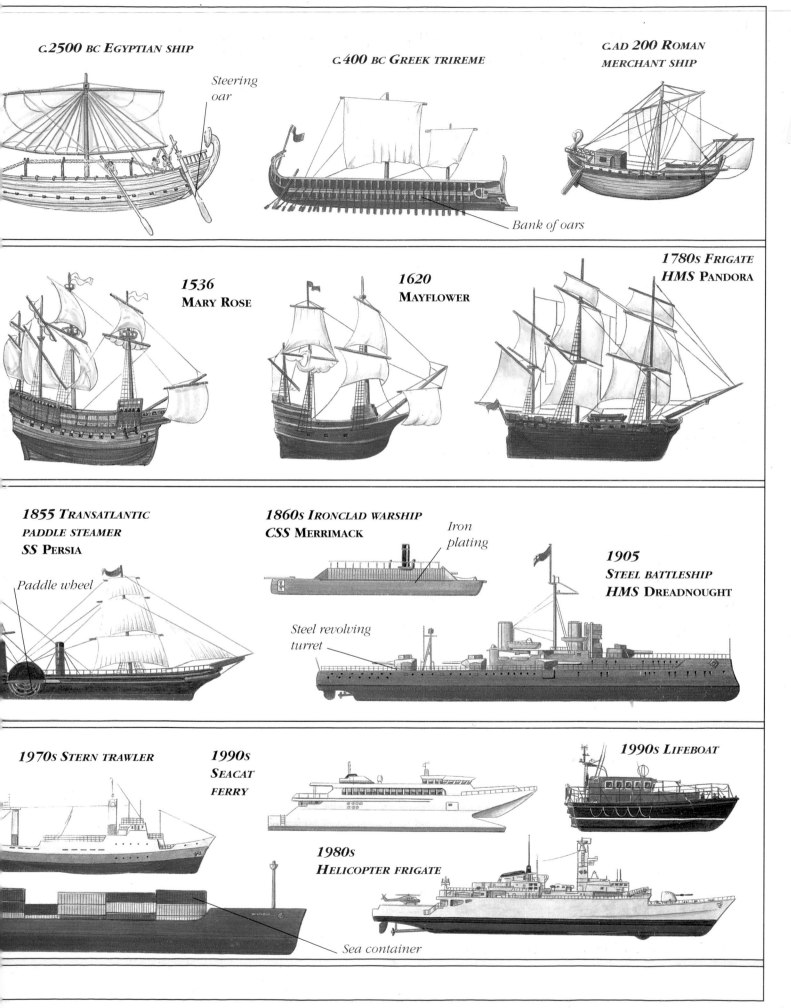

C.2500 BC EGYPTIAN SHIP

Steering oar

C.400 BC GREEK TRIREME

C.AD 200 ROMAN MERCHANT SHIP

Bank of oars

1780s FRIGATE HMS PANDORA

1536 MARY ROSE

1620 MAYFLOWER

1855 TRANSATLANTIC PADDLE STEAMER SS PERSIA

Paddle wheel

1860s IRONCLAD WARSHIP CSS MERRIMACK

Iron plating

Steel revolving turret

1905 STEEL BATTLESHIP HMS DREADNOUGHT

1970s STERN TRAWLER

1990s SEACAT FERRY

1990s LIFEBOAT

1980s HELICOPTER FRIGATE

Sea container

GLOSSARY

Aft
The area that is near or towards the back (stern) of the ship.

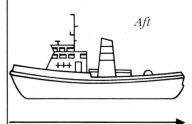

Aft

Amidships
The area in the middle of the ship.

Anchor
A heavy weight on the end of a thick rope or chain. It is thrown over the side and sticks in the seabed to stop the ship from drifting. When a ship is "anchored" it is stationary.

Anchor

Ballast
Weighty pieces of stone or cargo loaded into the bottom part of a ship to help balance it in water.

Bilge pump
A pump used to get rid of water that might have leaked inside the ship. Bilge pumps are usually put either side of the keel down in the broadest part of the hold, in the bottom of the ship. This area is called the bilge.

Boatswain
The foreman of a boat crew (usually shortened to Bo'sun).

Boiler
A water-tight container where water is turned into steam.

Bow
The front of a ship.

Bowsprit
A long spar sticking out from the front of a sailing ship. A bowsprit sail hangs here.

Bridge
An enclosed platform where the captain and helmsman stand on a modern ship. Orders are given from here.

Broadside
A volley of gunfire from one side of a ship.

Bulkhead
An inner wall which divides a ship into watertight sections.

Bulwark
The top part of the hull that runs around the ship above the upper deck.

Cabin
Living quarters for someone on board.

Capstan
A winding machine used to haul up heavy loads such as the anchor.

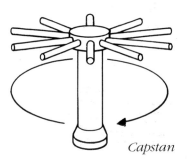

Capstan

Carvel built
A wooden hull where the planks are laid tightly edge to edge.

Clinker built
A wooden hull where the planks overlap each other.

Compass
An instrument with a magnetic needle that always points north. Sailors use it to find the way.

Deck
A platform that stretches across and along the boat.

Forecastle
(Usually shortened to fo'c'sle). A raised fighting platform at the front of a wooden ship. In a modern ship it is an area in the front part of the ship where the crew's cabins are usually found.

Foremast
The mast situated in front of the mainmast.

Forward
Towards the front of the boat.

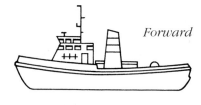

Forward

Frigate
A small warship.

Funnel
A large pipe used on steamships to carry off smoke and steam from the ship's engines. It is open to the sky at the top.

Galley
A ship's kitchen. Also a boat powered by rows of oarsmen.

Gunport
A hole cut in the side of a ship so that a gun such as a cannon can fire out of it.

Helmsman
The person who steers a ship.

Hold
The space inside the bottom of the ship. It is often used for storing cargo and provisions.

Hull
The outer shell of a ship.

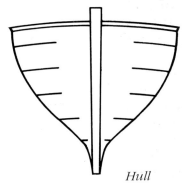

Hull

Junk
A Chinese boat with bamboo-ribbed sails.

Keel
A strong rib that runs all the way along underneath the hull. It is the backbone of the ship.

Knot
The measure of a ship's speed. One knot is one nautical mile per hour.

Mainmast
The pole stretching up from the deck in the middle of a sailing ship.

Man-of-war
A large, heavily-armed sailing warship of the 18th and 19th centuries.

Mate
A ship's officer under the captain.

Merchant ship
A ship used for carrying cargo, not for fighting.

Mizzen mast
The mast situated behind the mainmast.

Outrigger
An extension, built so that it sticks out of the side of a boat's hull.

Poopdeck
A high deck raised above the stern (back) of a ship.

Port
The left-hand side of a ship. It is also an order which means "turn to the left".

Propeller
Blades mounted on a shaft underneath the water at the back of a ship. It is also called a screw. Ship engines drive it round in the water. This pushes the ship forwards.

Propeller

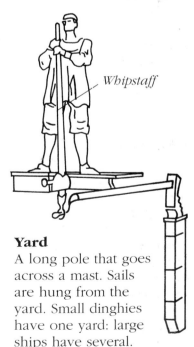

Prow
The part of a hull which sticks out at the very front of a wooden ship.

Quarterdeck
The raised deck situated towards the back of a sailing ship.

Radar
A revolving aerial that sends out invisible electromagnetic waves, which bounce off any objects they hit. The returning waves are measured by a radar scanner and the measurements show how far away the objects are. Sailors use radar to find other ships.

Ram
A long pointed piece that stuck out of the front of a wooden ship from underneath the waterline. It was designed to ram holes into enemy ships under the water.

Rigging
Ropes or wires used to hold up the sails and masts on a sailing ship.

Rudder
A large piece of timber or metal hinged to a post that fits into a ship at the back. The rudder is moved to the left or right to make the ship change direction.

Sail
A large sheet of canvas carried on the masts of a sailing ship used to harness the wind's power to drive the ship forwards. Sails were identified by the mast on which they were carried.

Sail

Shipwright
A shipbuilder.

Starboard
The right-hand side of a ship. It is also an order which means "turn to the right".

Stem
Narrowest point at the very front of a ship, which parts the water as the ship moves forwards.

Stern
The back of a ship.

Tiller
A part inside a boat that is attached to the rudder outside. When the tiller is moved, the rudder moves.

Tiller   *Rudder*

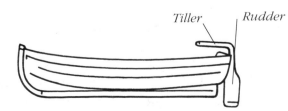

Trireme
An ancient Greek boat powered by three rows of oarsmen.

Waterline
The water level along the side of a ship.

Wheel
The ship's wheel is turned to move the rudder and steer the vessel.

Wheel

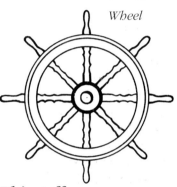

Whipstaff
A giant lever attached to the tiller on an old wooden ship. Before ships had steering wheels the sailors swung the whipstaff to make the rudder move.

Whipstaff

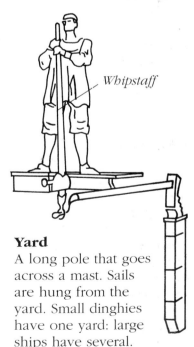

Yard
A long pole that goes across a mast. Sails are hung from the yard. Small dinghies have one yard; large ships have several.

INDEX

A

aircraft carrier, 18-21
anchor, stockless, 24
anti-aircraft (AA) guns, 18
archers, 9
armour plating, 14, 21
arrestor cables, 21

B

battleship, 14-15
HMS *Bounty*, 12-13
bulkheads, 23

C

SS *Canberra*, 16-17
cannons, 8
captain, 13, 17
carrack, 8
carriage guns, 8
carronades, 13
carvel planking, 8
castles, 8
cell, 13
Chinese junk, 22-23
clinker planking, 8
compass, 27
crewmen, 12, 17

D

decks, 12, 17;
   see also flight deck,
   hangar deck
HMS *Dreadnought*, 14-15

E

engines *see* steam turbine
   engines
eye, painted, 6, 22

F

fighting tops, 8
figurehead, 12
fire director
   HMS *Dreadnought*, 15

USS *Lexington*, 19, 20
fish-washing machine, 25
fishing boat, 24-25
fishing nets, 24, 25
flight deck, 18
forecastle (fo'c'sle), 8, 12
frigate, 12

G

gimballed compass, 27
gun sighting device, *see*
   fire director
gun turret, 21
gunports, 8
guns
   HMS *Dreadnought* , 15
   USS *Lexington*, 18, 21
   Mary Rose, 8-9
   Mayflower ,11
   HMS *Pandora*, 12, 13

H

hangar deck, 19
house, 23
hull, 16, 26
hypozoma, 7

I

island, 19; *see also*
   superstructure

J

junk, 22-23

K

Kamikaze suicide
   planes, 18

L

USS *Lexington*, 18-21
life rocket, 26
lifebelts, 26
lifeboats, 16, 26-27

M

Mary Rose, 8-9
masts
   Mary Rose, 8
   Mayflower, 10
   trireme, 6
Mayflower, 10-11
merchant ship, 10-11

N

nets/netting
   HMS *Dreadnought*, 14
   lifeboat, 26
   Mary Rose, 9
   trawler, 24, 25

O

oarsmen, 6
ocean liner, 16-17
officers, 13
oilskins, 26
otter boards, 25

P

HMS *Pandora*, 12-13
passenger cabins, 16
pilgrims, 10-11
pinnace, 14
planking, 8
prisoners, 13
propellers, 16

Q

quarterdeck, 13

R

radar, 20, 27
radio aerials, 20
ram, 6
RNLI, 26, 27
rudder, 22, 23

S

sails
   Mayflower, 10
   trireme, 6
soldiers, 9
steam catapult, 18
steam pinnace, 14
steam turbine engines
   SS *Canberra*, 16
   HMS *Dreadnought*, 14
   USS *Lexington*, 20
stern trawler, 24
sterncastle, 8
stockless anchor, 24
superstructure, 17; *see*
   also island

T

toilets, 10
torpedoes, 14
trawl, 24
trawler, 24-25
trireme, 6-7

W

warships
   USS *Lexington*, 18-21
   Mary Rose, 8-9
   HMS *Pandora*, 12-13
watertight compartments, 21,
   22, 23
weapons, 9; *see also* guns
whipstaff, 11

Acknowledgements

Dorling Kindersley would like
to thank the following people
who helped in the preparation
of this book:

Constance Novis for editorial
support
Lynn Bresler for the index
Additional artwork by Chris Lyon
(page 14-15, 18-21), Roger Stewart
(page 16-17) and Brihton
Illustration (page 28-29)
Line artworks by John See